**BIG-NOTE PIANO**

*Walt Disney* PICTURES

PRESENTS

# Beauty

## and the Beast

### Arranged by Bill Boyd

Artwork © The Walt Disney Company

ISBN 0-7935-1435-5

**HAL•LEONARD®**
**CORPORATION**

7777 W. BLUEMOUND RD. P.O. BOX 13819 MILWAUKEE, WI 53213

# BELLE

Lyrics by HOWARD ASHMAN
Music by ALAN MENKEN

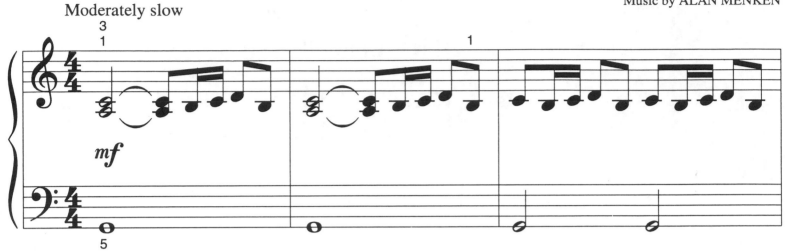

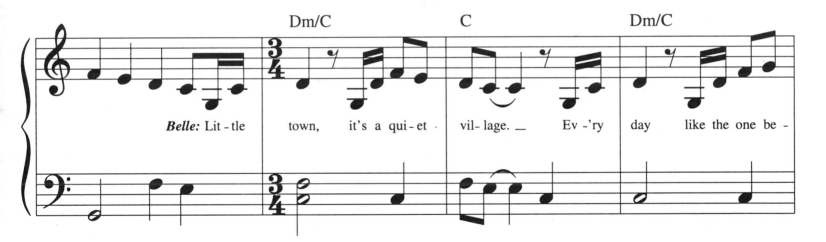

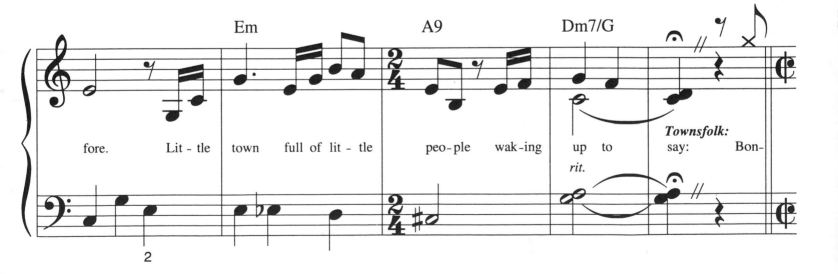

**Moderately**

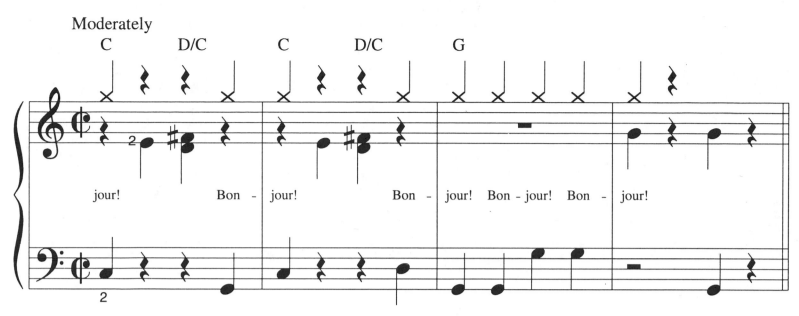

jour! Bon - jour! Bon - jour! Bon - jour! Bon - jour!

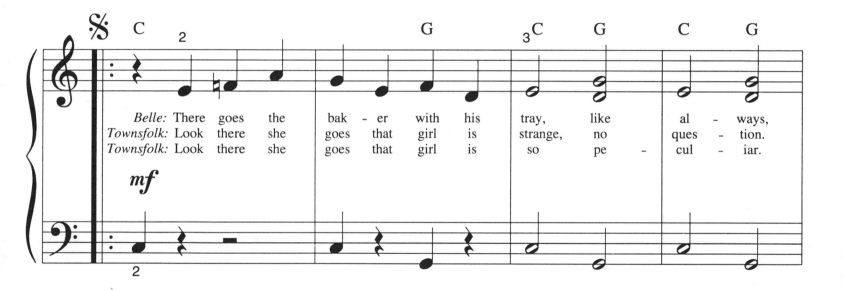

*mf*

*Belle:* There goes the bak - er with his tray, like al - ways,
*Townsfolk:* Look there she goes that girl is strange, no ques - tion.
*Townsfolk:* Look there she goes that girl is so pe - cul - iar.

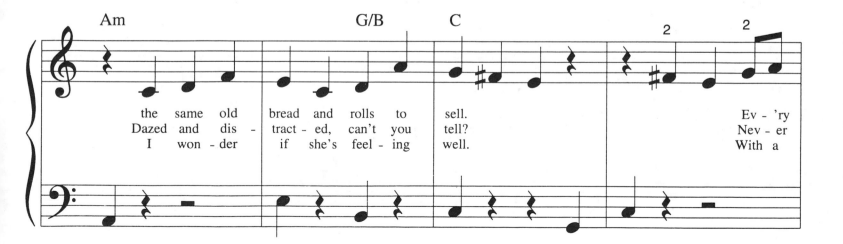

the same old bread and rolls to sell. Ev - 'ry
Dazed and dis - tract - ed, can't you tell? Nev - er
I won - der if she's feel - ing well. With a

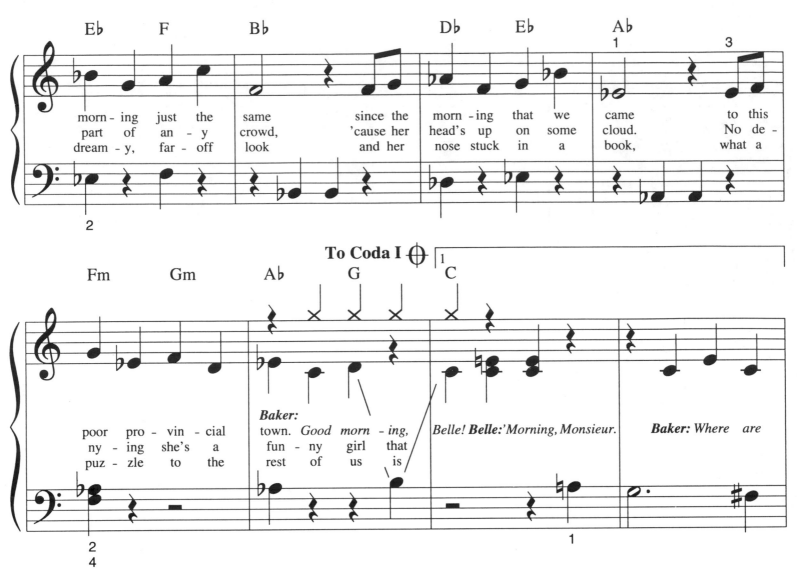

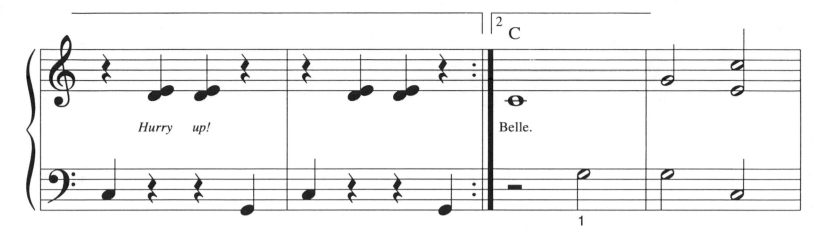

*Hurry up!* ... Belle.

F G F G F G/F C/E

*Man I:* Bon - jour. *Woman I:* Good day. *Man I:* How is your fam - 'ly?

F G F G F G/F C/E

*Woman II:* Bon - jour. *Man II:* Good day. *Woman II:* How is your wife?

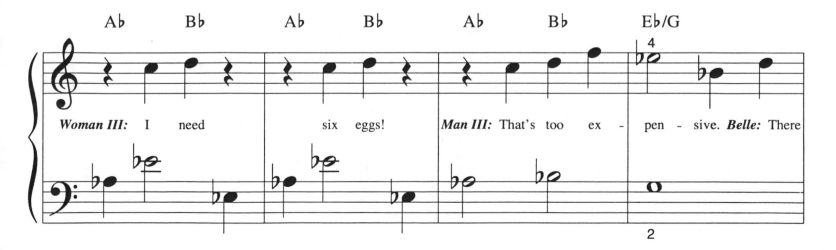

A♭ B♭ A♭ B♭ A♭ B♭ E♭/G

*Woman III:* I need six eggs! *Man III:* That's too ex - pen - sive. *Belle:* There

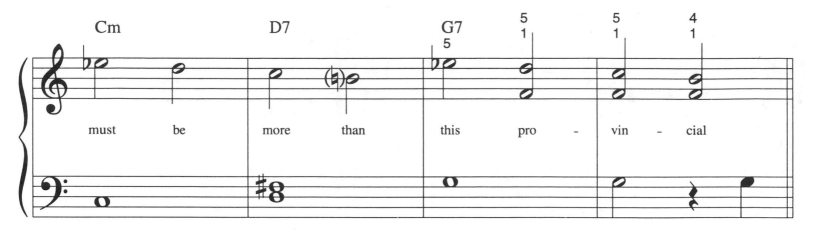

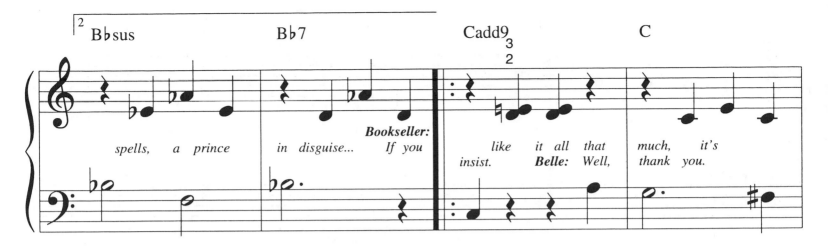

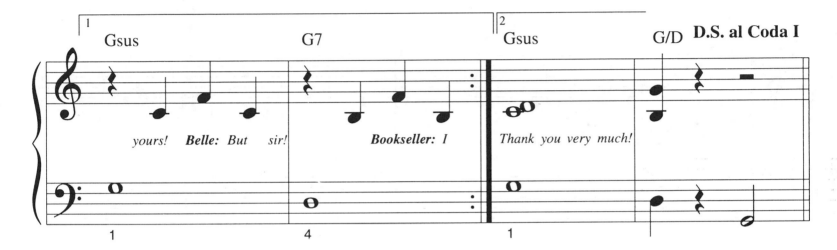

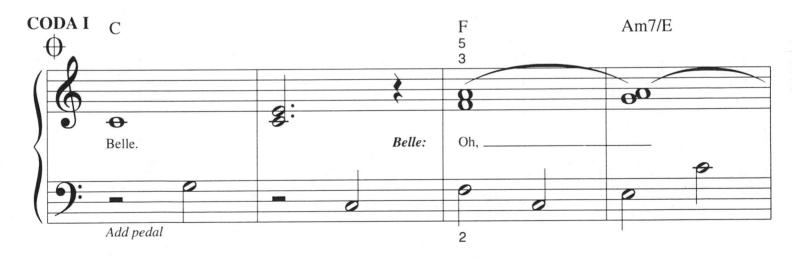

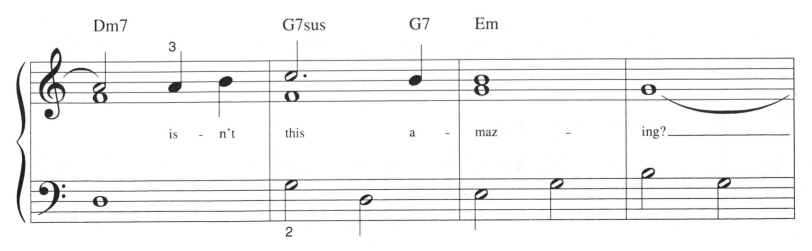

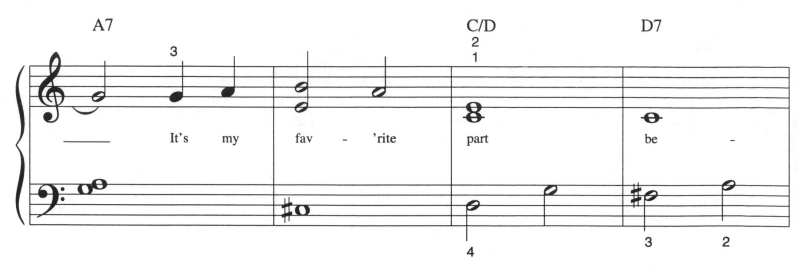

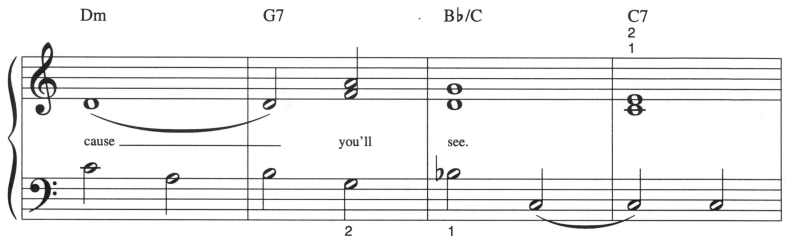

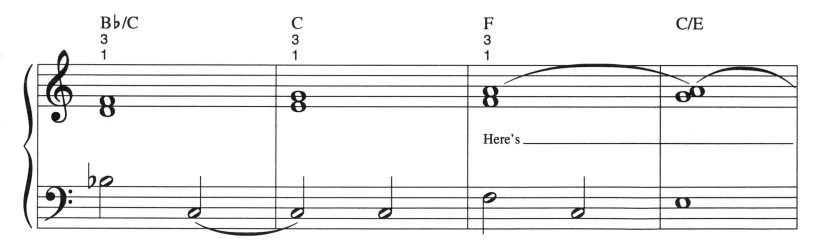

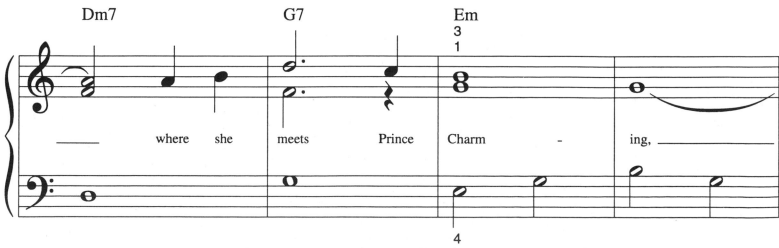

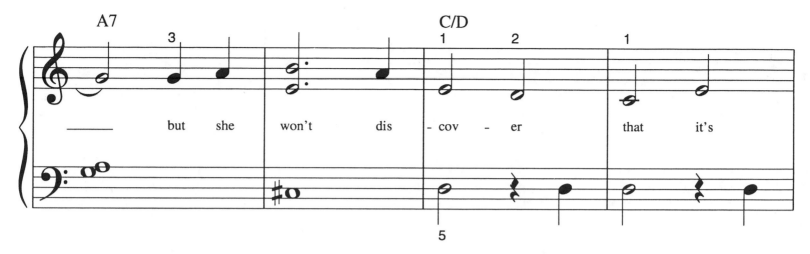

but she won't dis — cov — er that it's

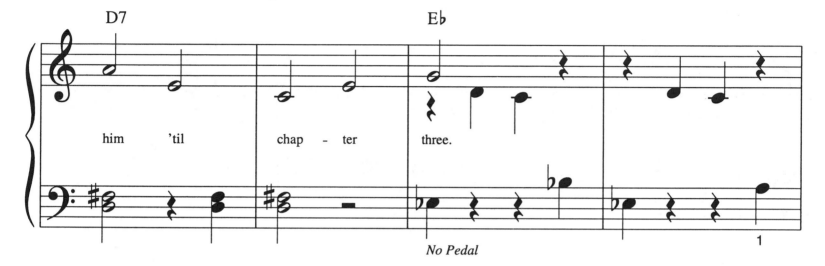

him 'til chap — ter three.

*No Pedal*

**Woman:** Now, it's no won — der that her
**Townsfolk:** Look there she goes a girl who's

name means "beau — ty."
strange but spe — cial.

Her looks have got no par — al —
A most pe — cu — liar mad — 'moi —

**To Coda II** ⊕ ⊕

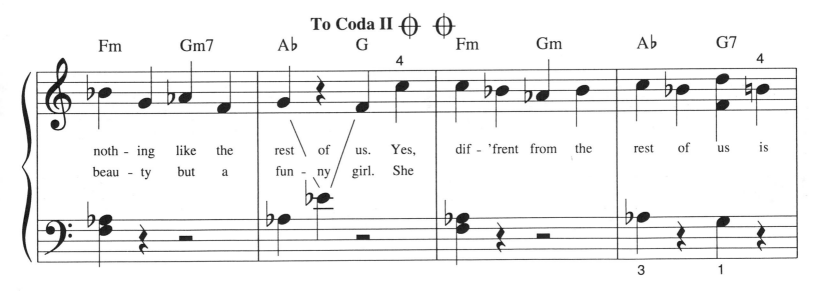

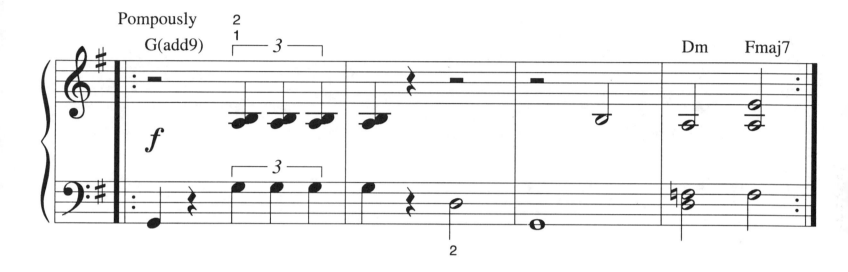

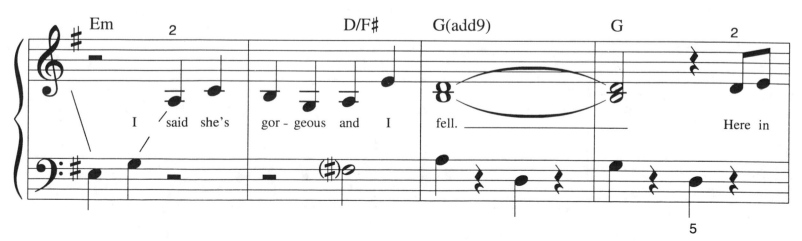

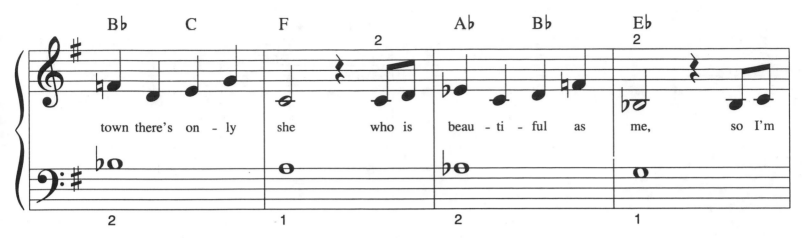

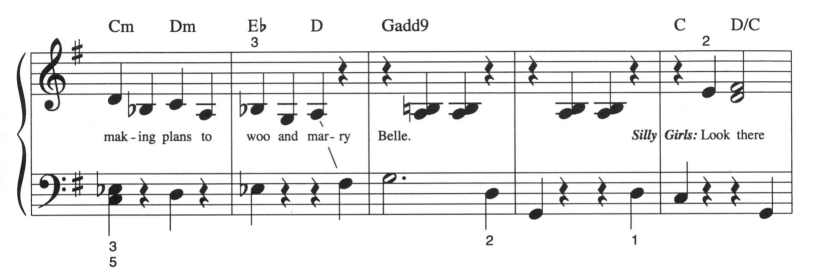

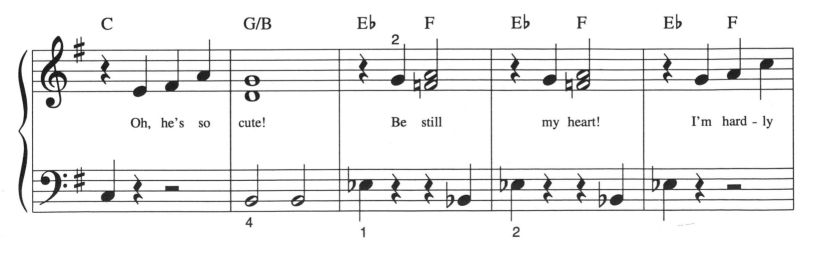

14

more than this pro - vin - cial life! *Gaston:* Just watch, I'm go - ing to make

**D.S.S. al Coda II**

**CODA II**

Belle my wife!

real - ly is a fun - ny girl

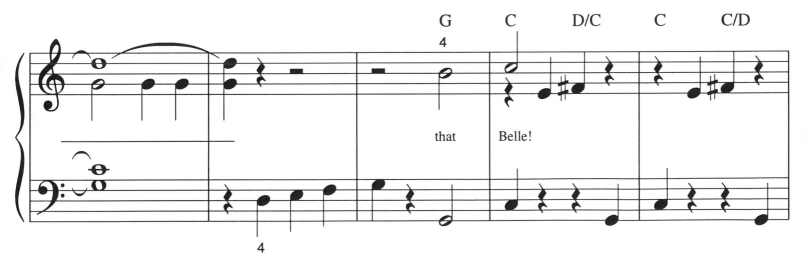

that Belle!

# BELLE
## (Reprise)

Lyrics by HOWARD ASHMAN
Music by ALAN MENKEN

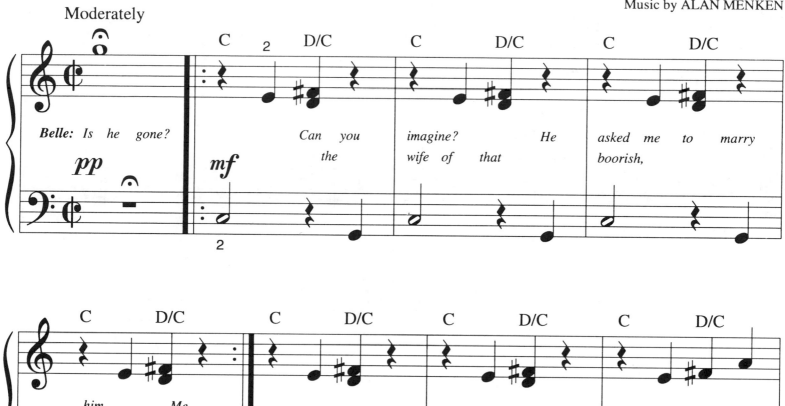

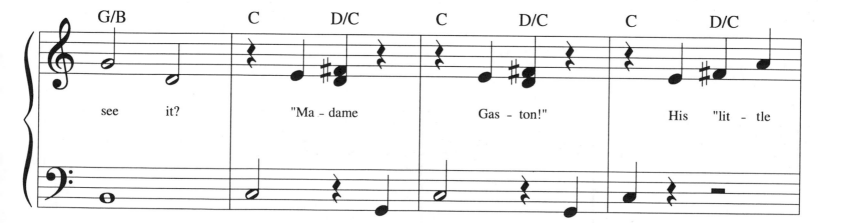

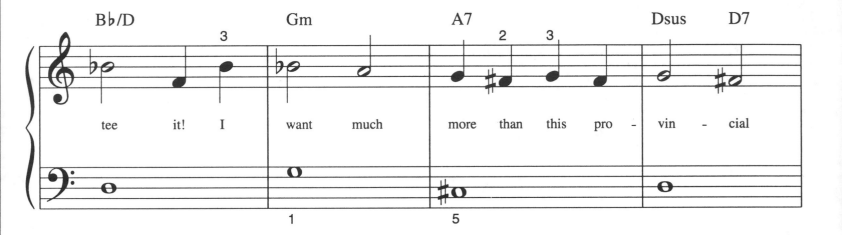

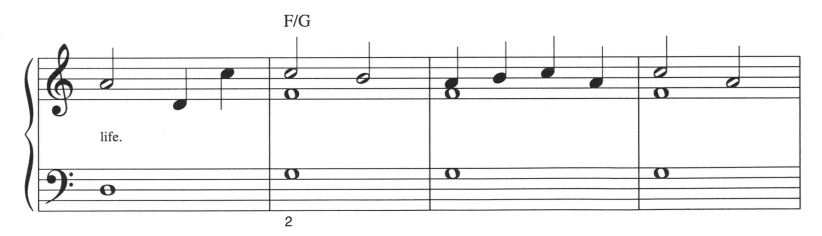

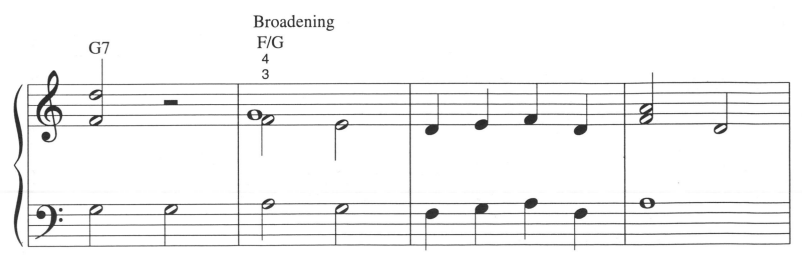

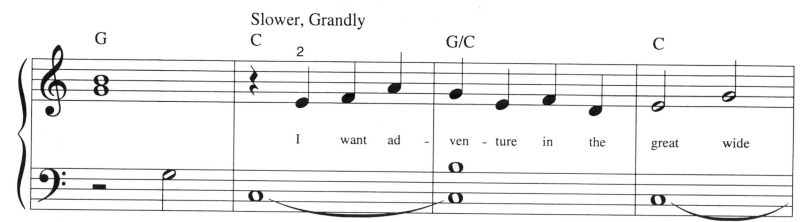

**Slower, Grandly**

I want ad - ven - ture in the great wide some - where!

I want it more than I can tell!

**Freely**

And for once it might be grand to have some - one un - der -

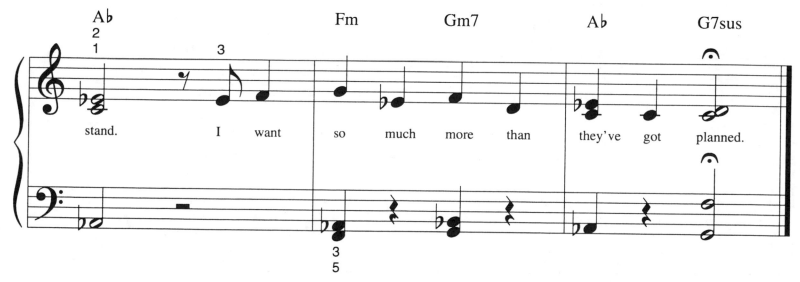

stand. I want so much more than they've got planned.

# GASTON

Lyrics by HOWARD ASHMAN
Music by ALAN MENKEN

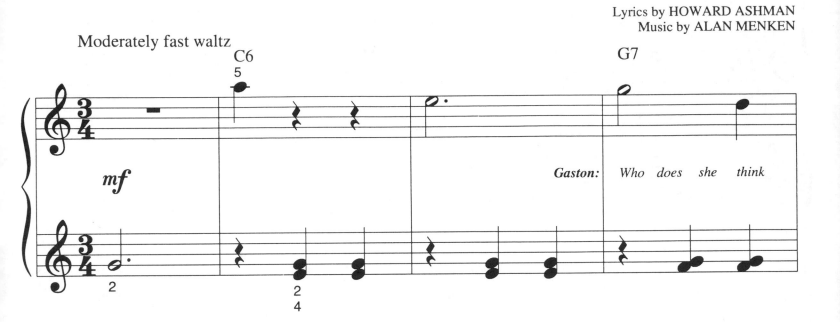

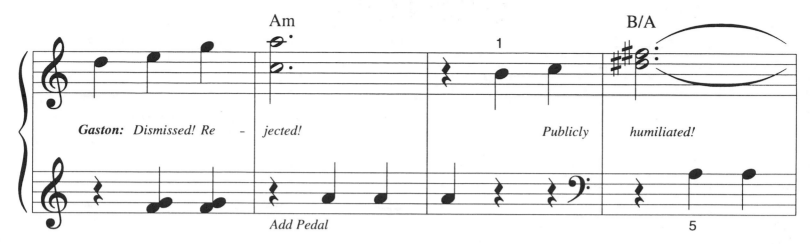

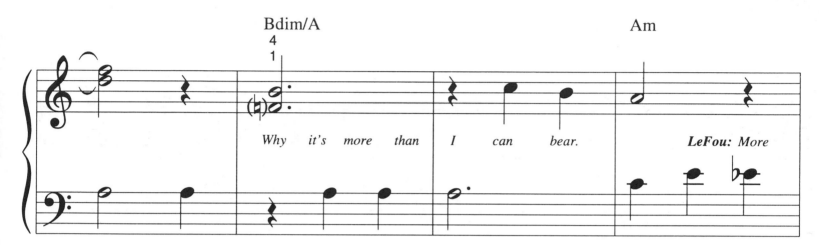

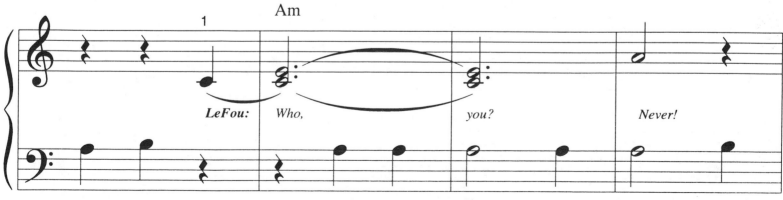

_Gaston,_ _you've_ _got_ _to_ _pull_ _yourself_ _together._

**LeFou:** Gosh it dis - turbs me to see you, Gas -

_Add pedal_

B/A

Bdim/A                                      Asus

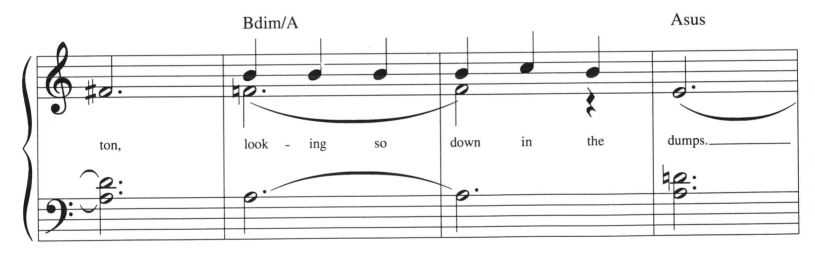

ton, look - ing so down in the dumps.

Am                                              B/A

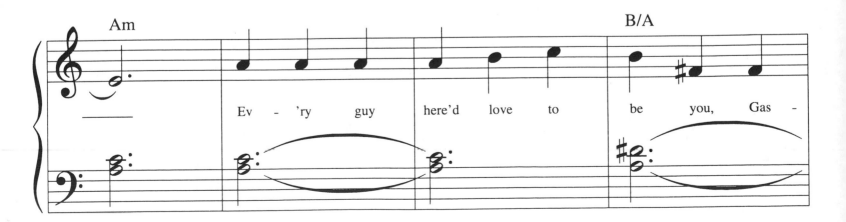

Ev - 'ry guy here'd love to be you, Gas -

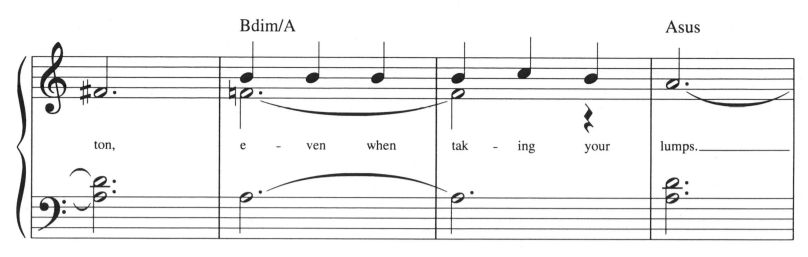

ton, e - ven when tak - ing your lumps.

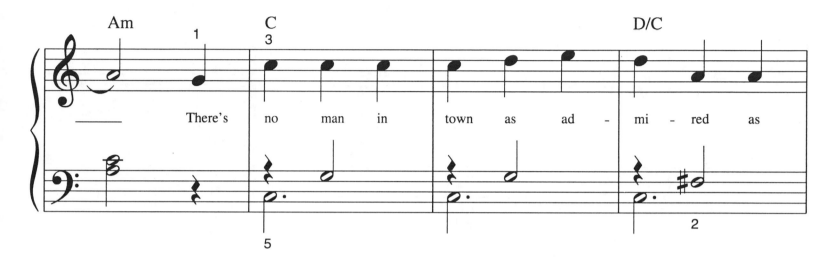

There's no man in town as ad - mi - red as

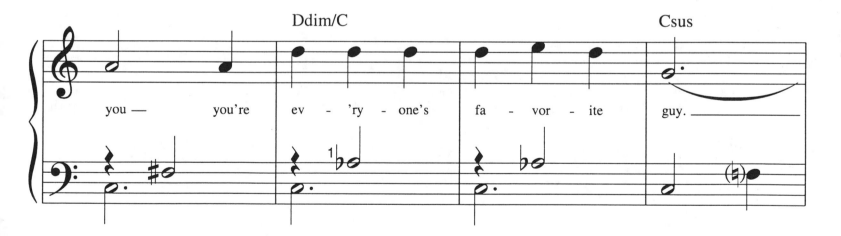

you — you're ev - 'ry - one's fa - vor - ite guy.

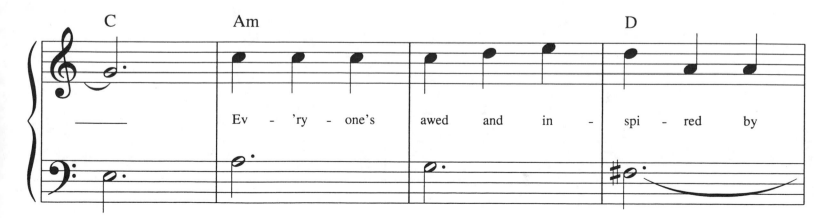

Ev - 'ry - one's awed and in - spi - red by

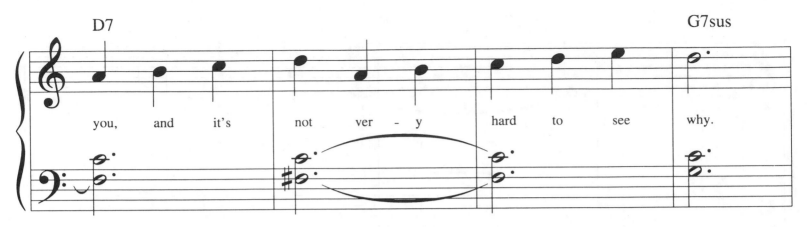

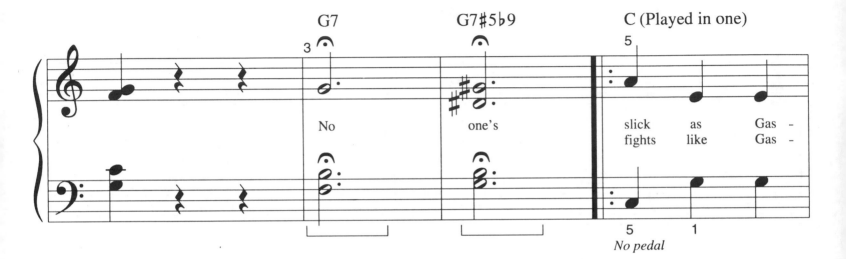

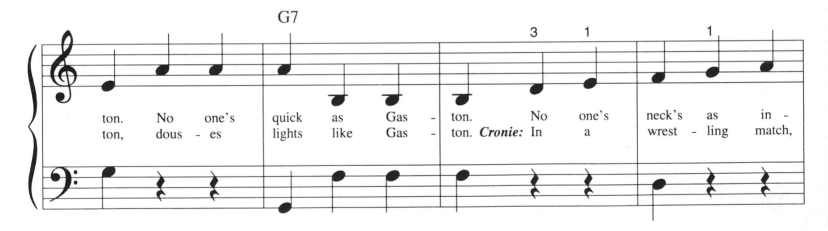

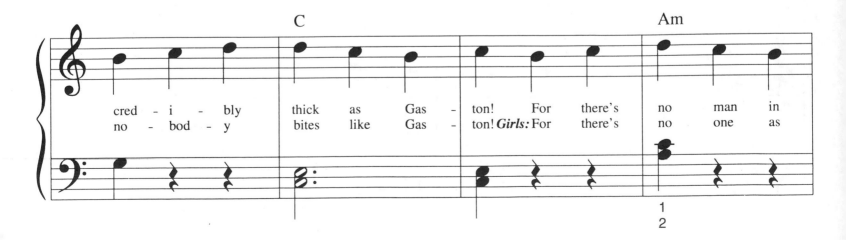

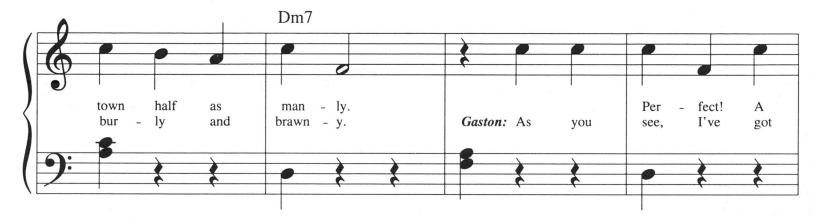

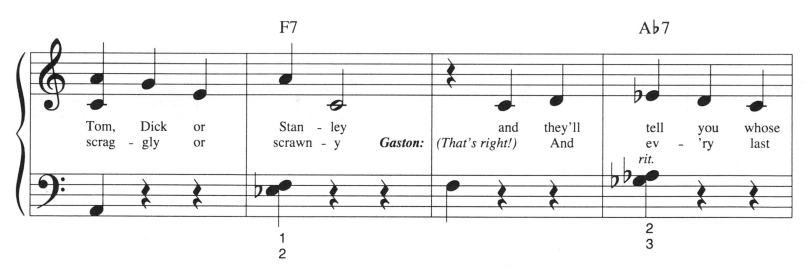

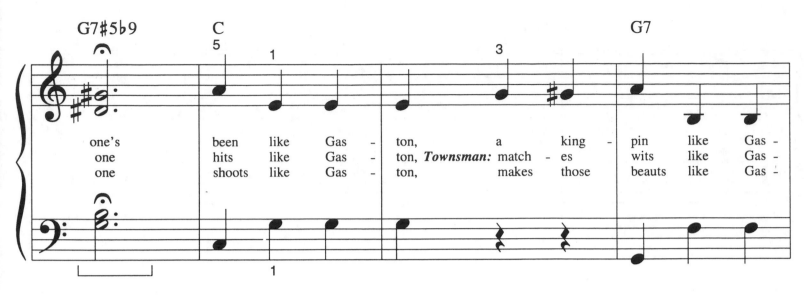

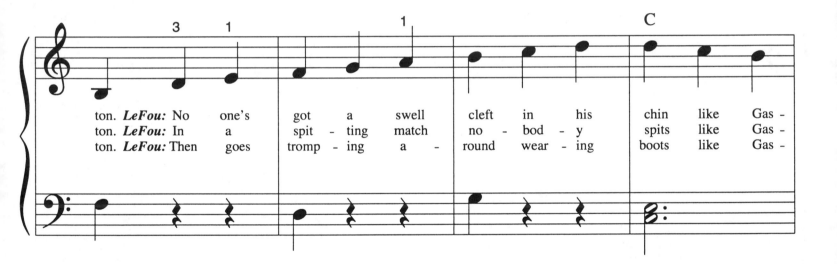

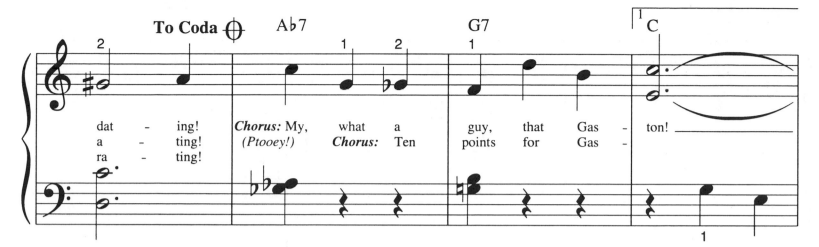

To Coda ⊕  A♭7  G7  [1.] C

dat - ing!  **Chorus:** My, what a guy, that Gas - ton! _____
a - ting!  (Ptooey!) **Chorus:** Ten points for Gas -
ra - ting!

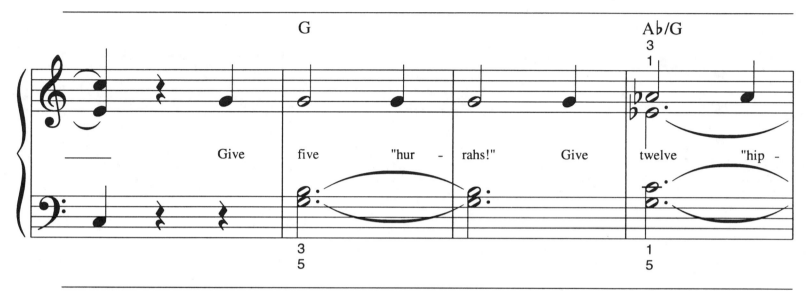

G  A♭/G

_____ Give five "hur - rahs!" Give twelve "hip -

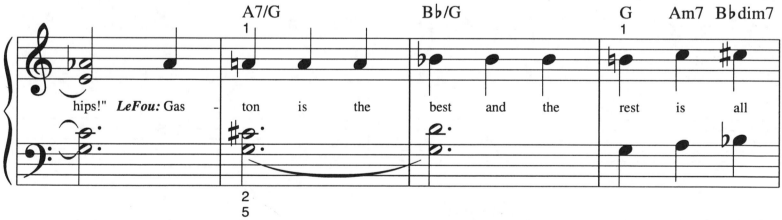

A7/G  B♭/G  G  Am7  B♭dim7

hips!" **LeFou:** Gas - ton is the best and the rest is all

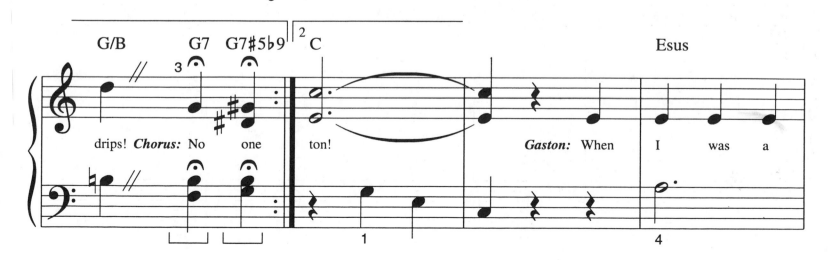

G/B  G7  G7#5♭9  [2.] C  Esus

drips! **Chorus:** No one ton! **Gaston:** When I was a

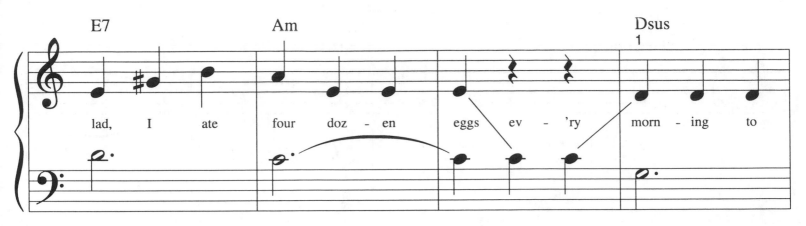

lad, I ate four doz - en eggs ev - 'ry morn - ing to

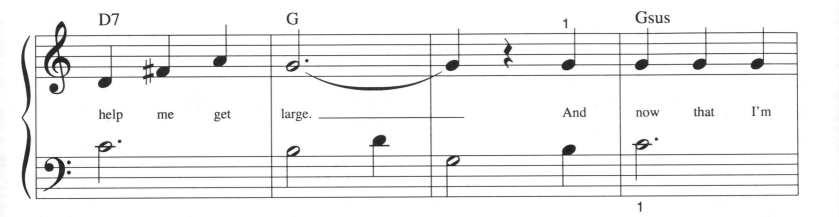

help me get large. _____ And now that I'm

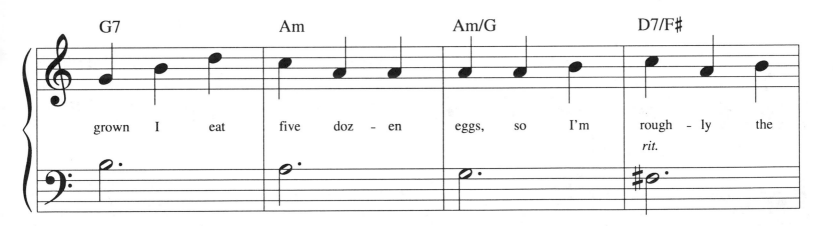

grown I eat five doz - en eggs, so I'm rough - ly the
*rit.*

**D.S. al Coda**

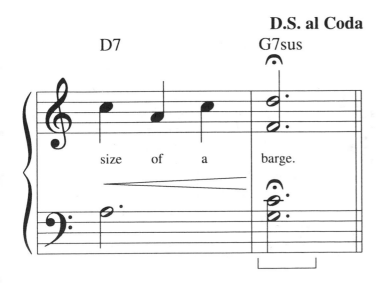

size of a barge.

**CODA** C/G

*Chorus:* Say it a - gain. Who's a

man a - mong men? And then say it once more. Who's the

he - ro next door? Who's a su - per suc - cess? Don't you

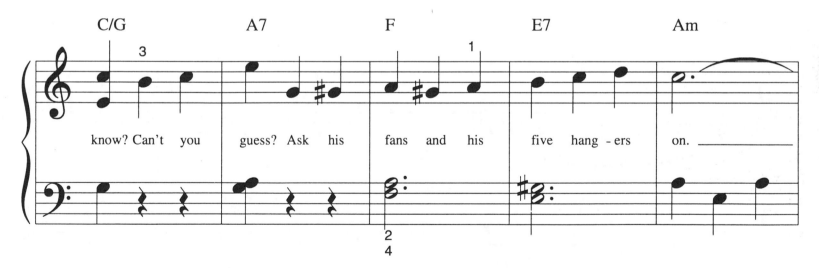

know? Can't you guess? Ask his fans and his five hang - ers on. _____

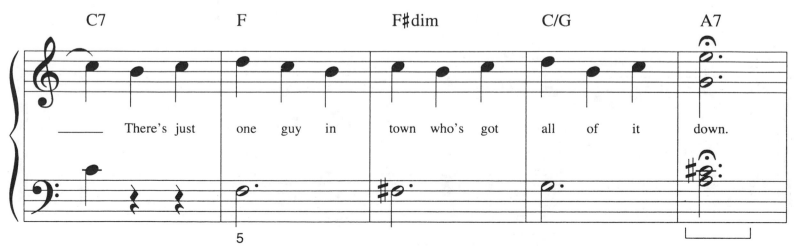

_____ There's just one guy in town who's got all of it down.

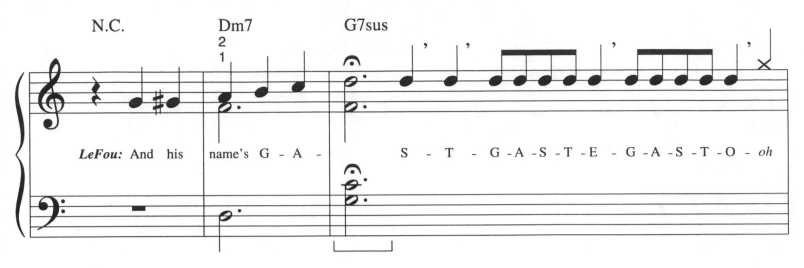

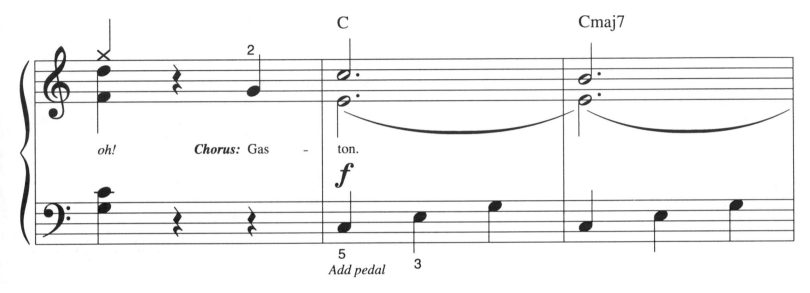

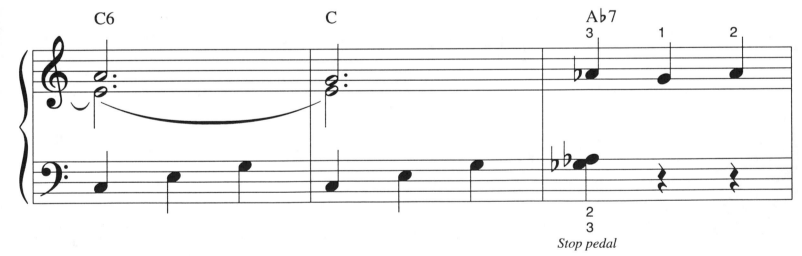

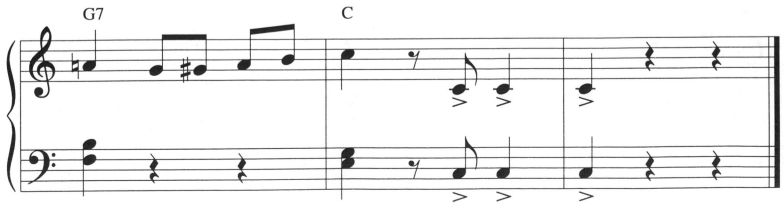

# GASTON
## (Reprise)

Lyrics by HOWARD ASHMAN
Music by ALAN MENKEN

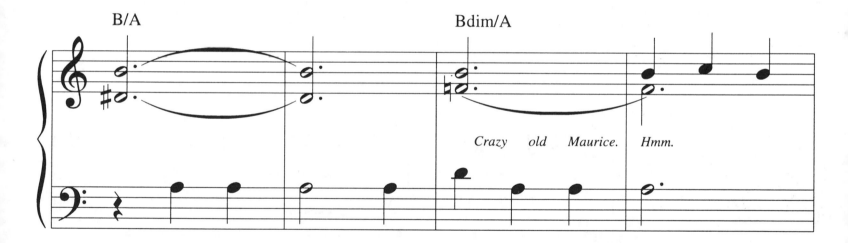

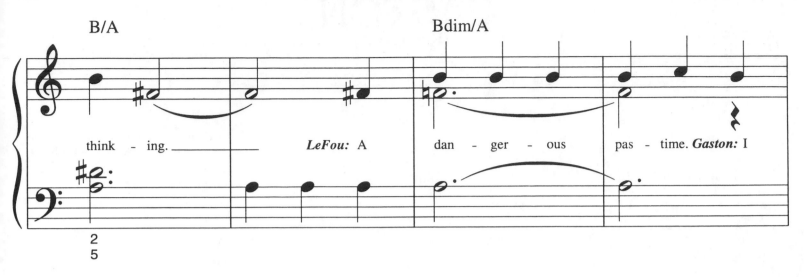

B/A    Bdim/A

think - ing. _____    *LeFou:* A    dan - ger - ous    pas - time. *Gaston:* I

25

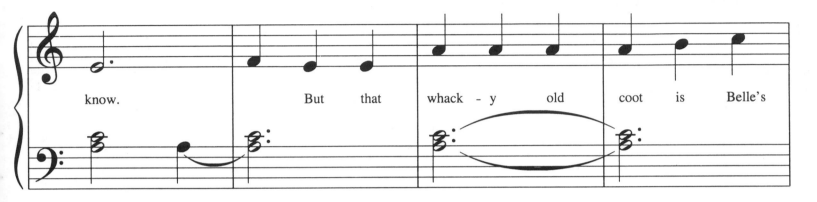

know.    But that    whack - y old    coot is Belle's

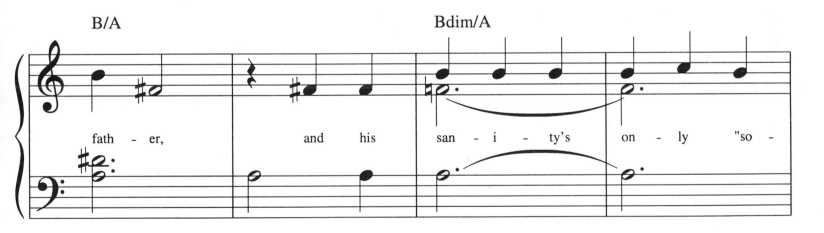

B/A    Bdim/A

fath - er,    and his    san - i - ty's    on - ly "so -

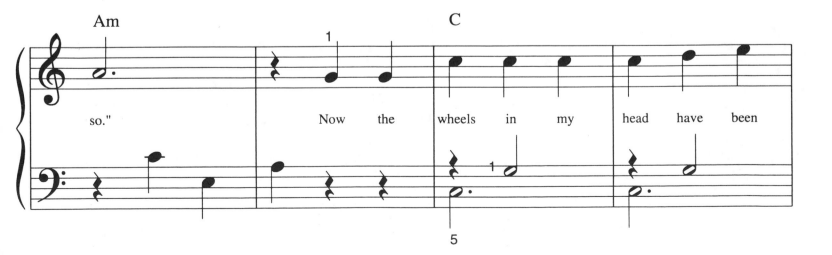

Am    C

so."    Now the    wheels in my    head have been

5

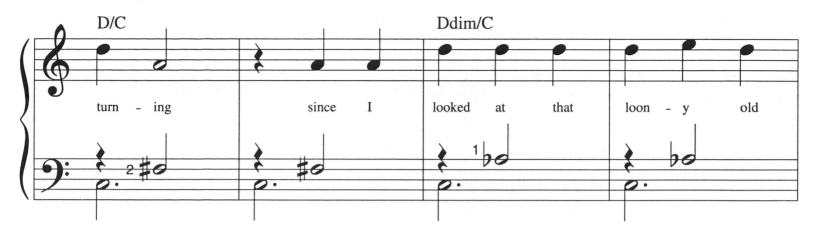

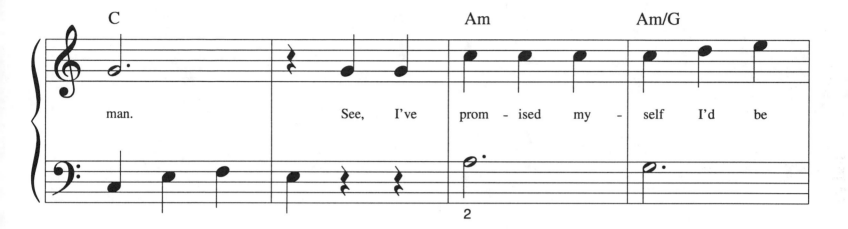

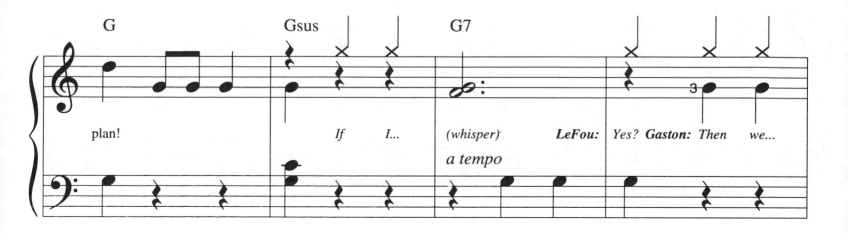

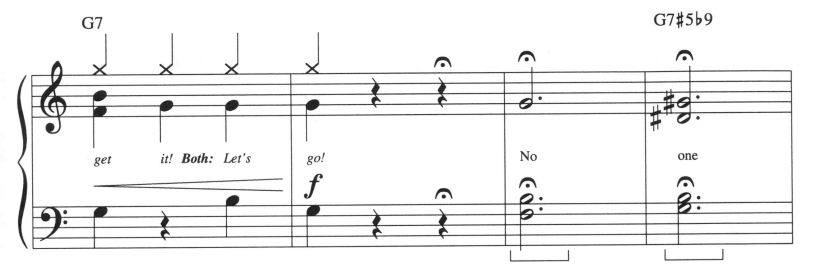

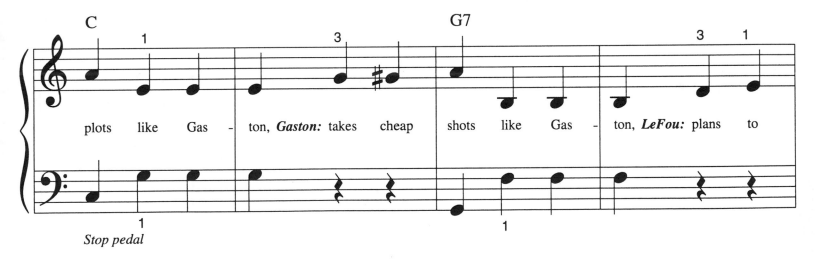

Stop pedal

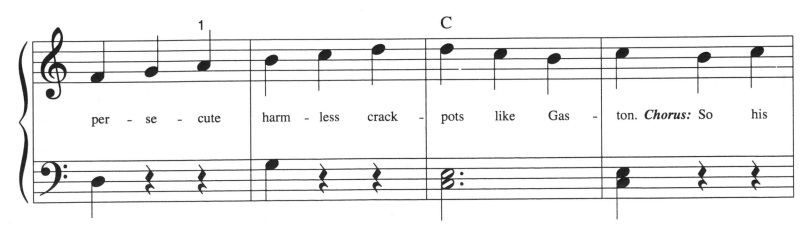

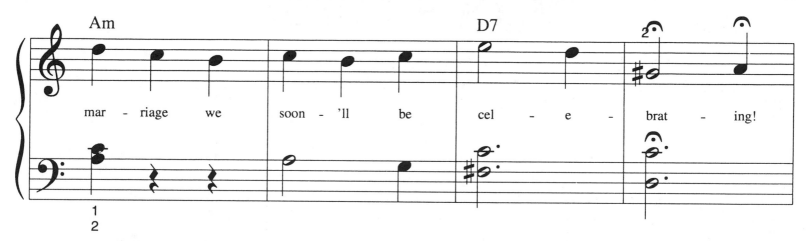

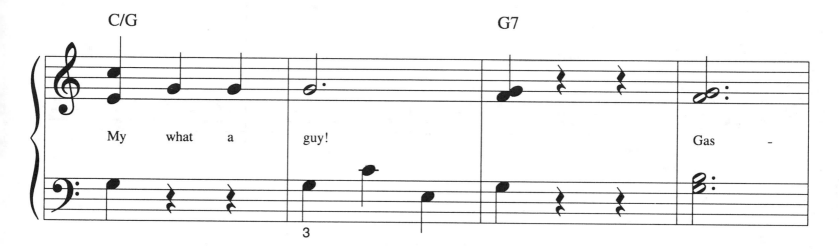

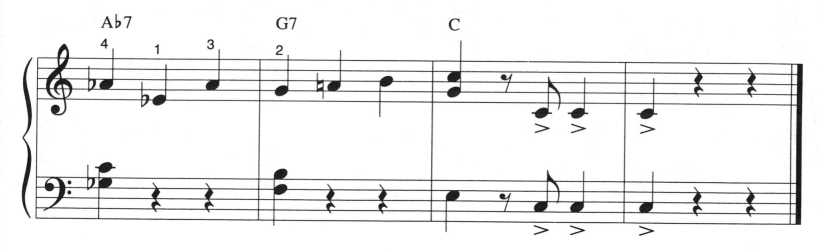

# BE OUR GUEST

Lyrics by HOWARD ASHMAN
Music by ALAN MENKEN

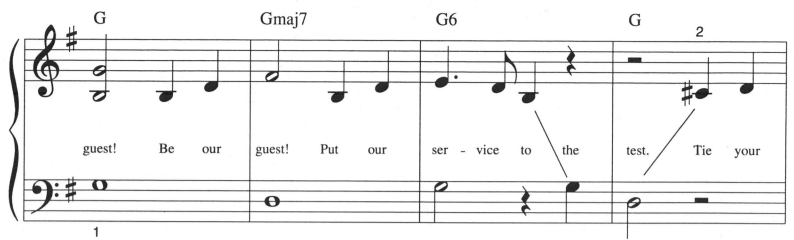

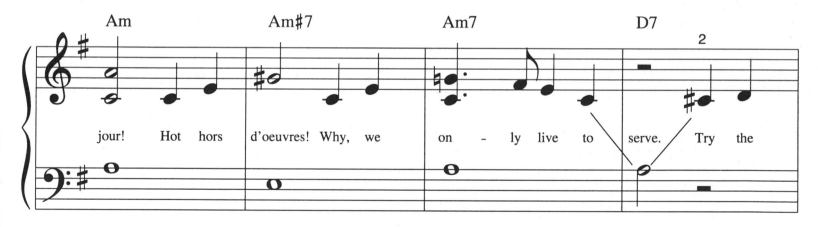

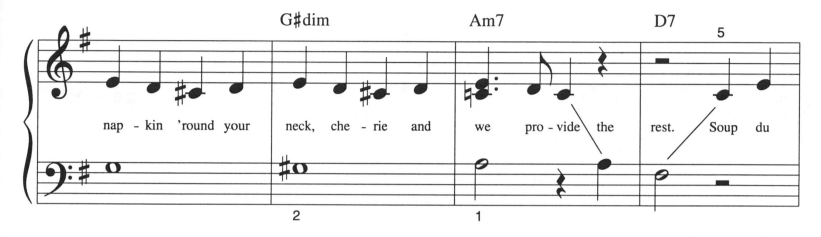

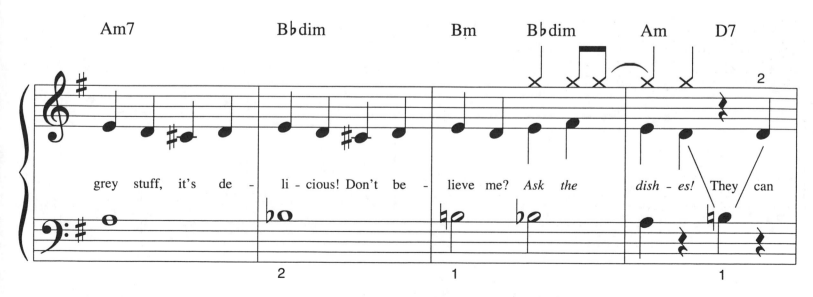

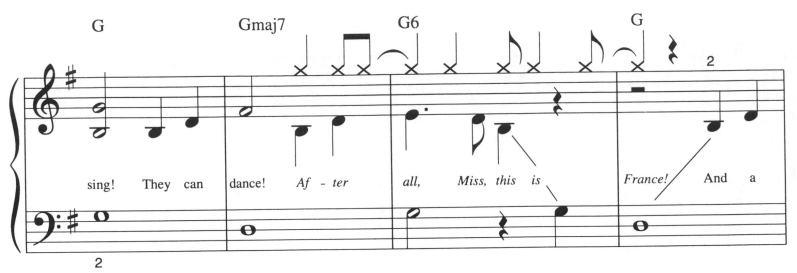

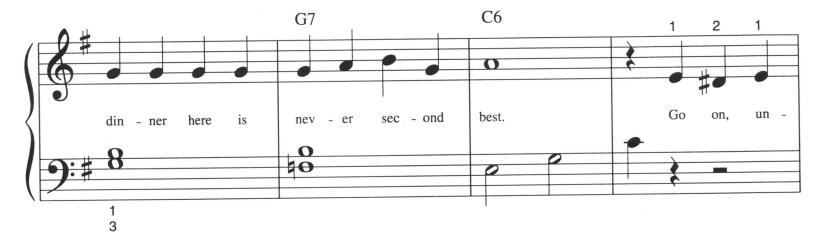

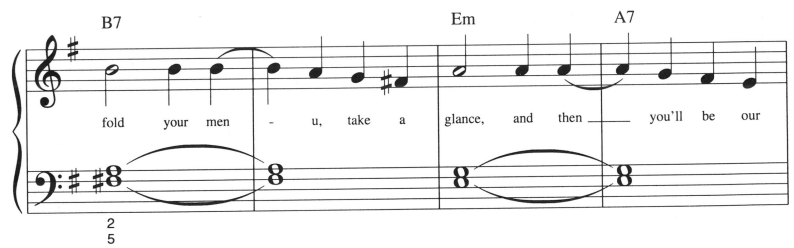

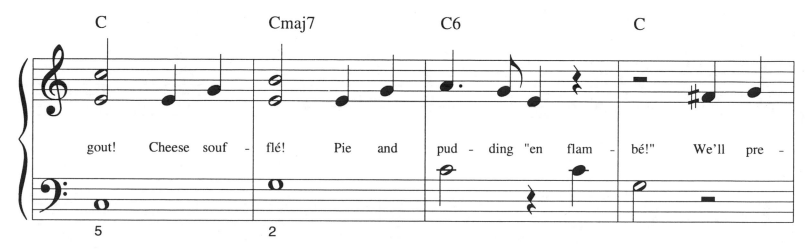

gout! Cheese souf - flé! Pie and pud - ding "en flam - bé!" We'll pre -

pare and serve with flair a cu - li - na - ry ca - ba - ret. You're a -

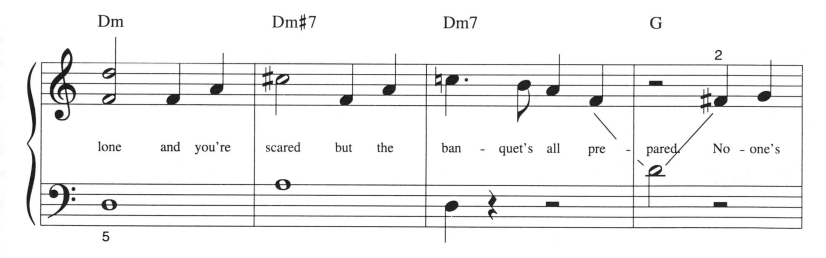

lone and you're scared but the ban - quet's all pre - pared. No - one's

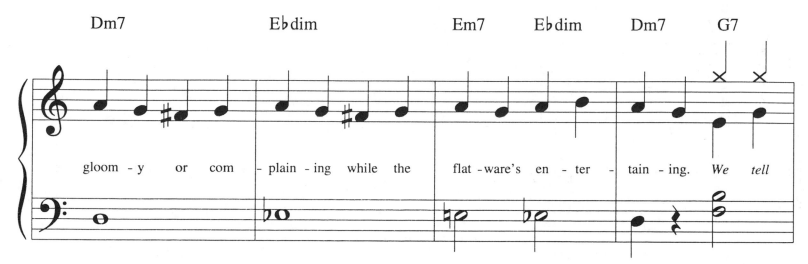

gloom - y or com - plain - ing while the flat - ware's en - ter - tain - ing. *We tell*

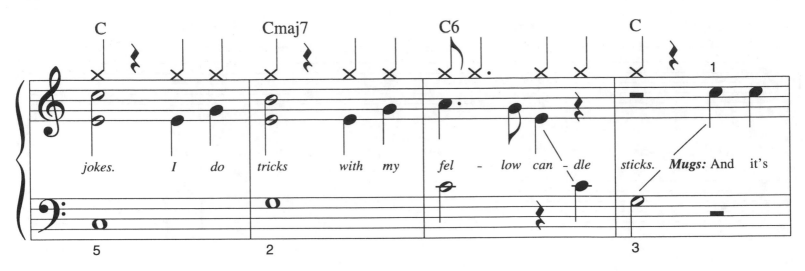

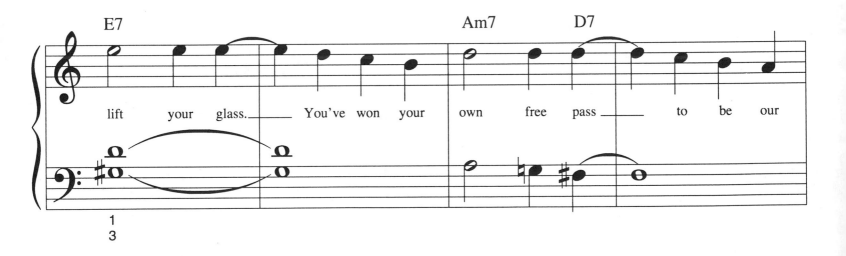

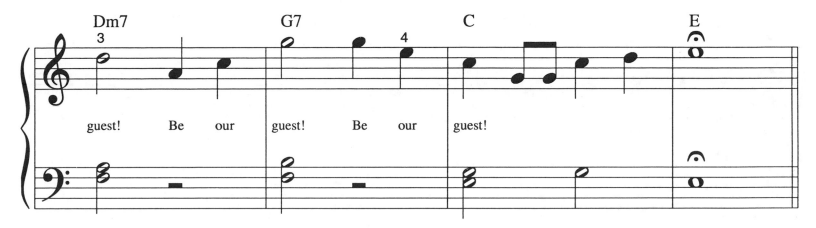

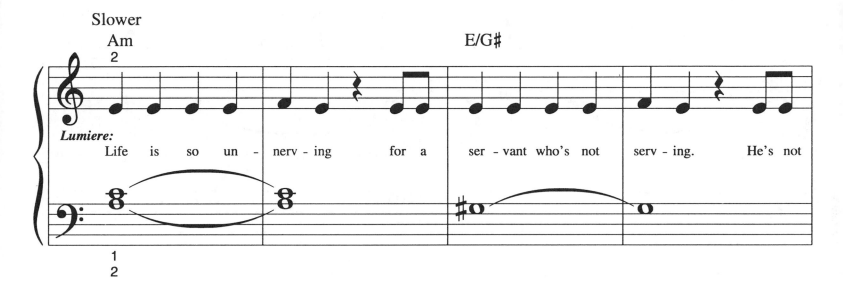

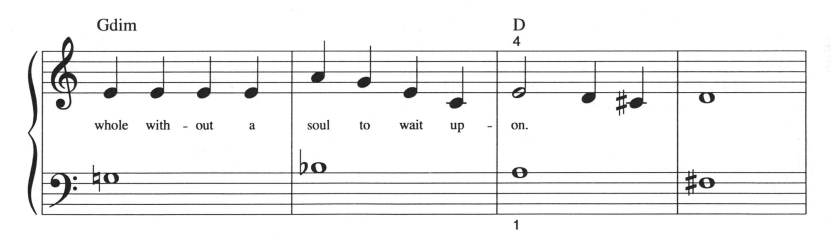

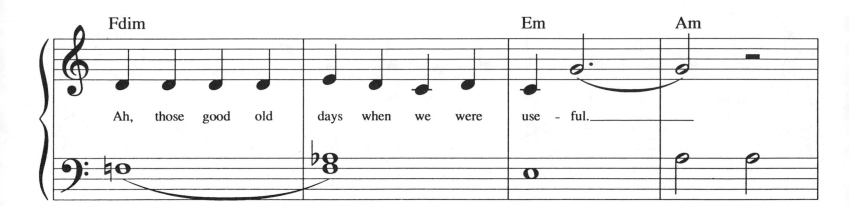

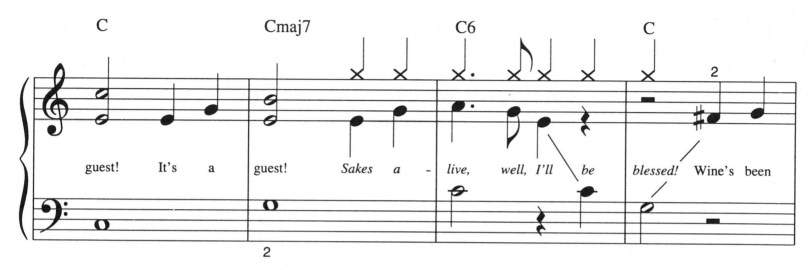

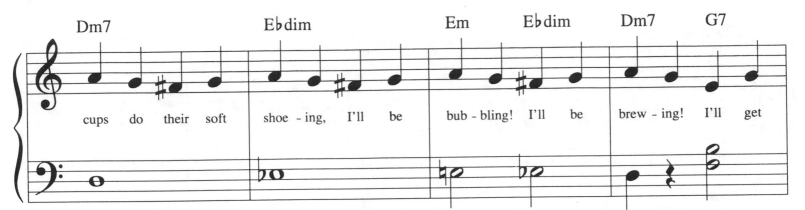

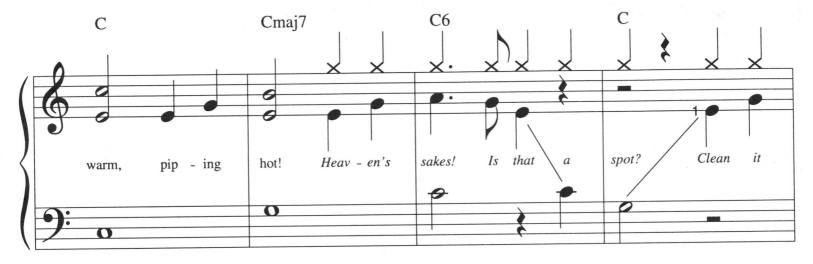

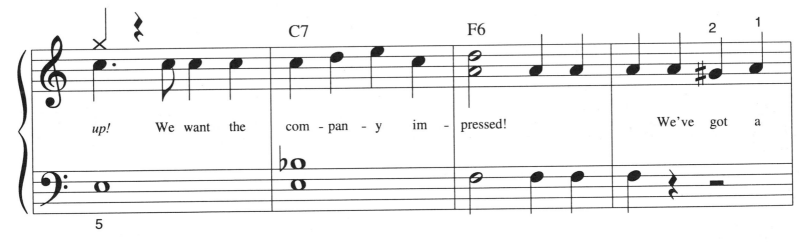

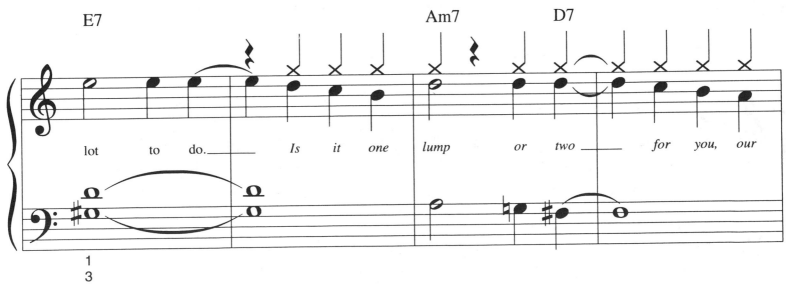

**Dm7** | **G7** | **Em** | **D7**

*Chorus:*
guest, She's our | *Mrs. Potts:* guest! She's our | *Chorus:* guest! She's our | guest! Be our

**G** | **Gmaj7** | **G6** | **G**

guest! Be our | guest! Our com- | -mand is your re- | quest. It's ten

**G♯dim** | **Am7** | **D7**

years since we had | an-y-bod-y | here, *and we're ob-* | *sessed.* With your

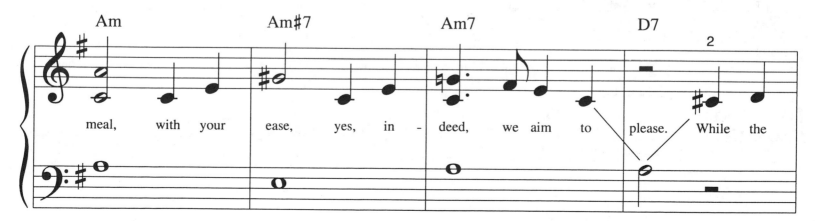

**Am** | **Am♯7** | **Am7** | **D7**

meal, with your | ease, yes, in- | deed, we aim to | please. While the

can - dle - light's still glow - ing let us help you, we'll keep go - ing course by

**Much slower**

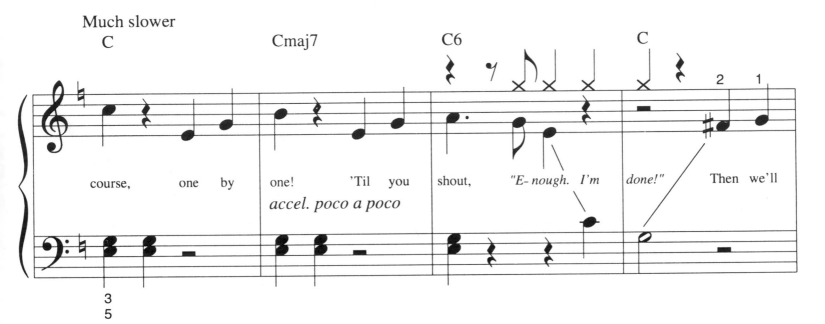

course, one by one! 'Til you shout, *"E- nough. I'm done!"* Then we'll

*accel. poco a poco*

sing you off to sleep as you di - gest. To - night you'll

**A Tempo**

prop your feet ___ up! But for now, let's eat ___ up! Be our

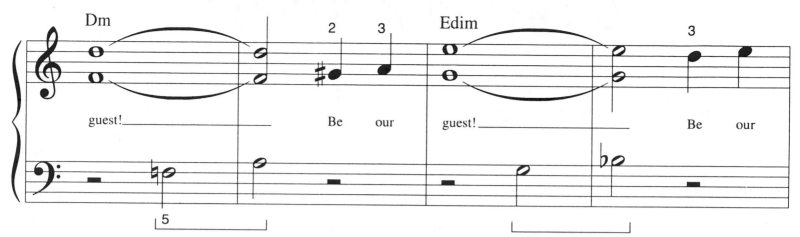

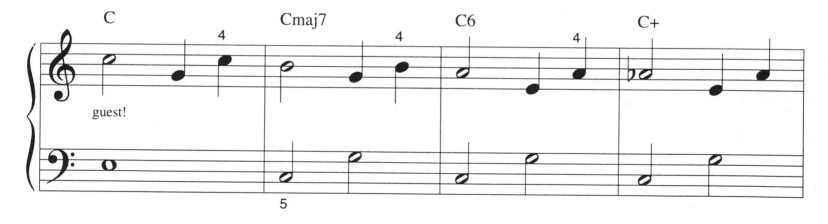

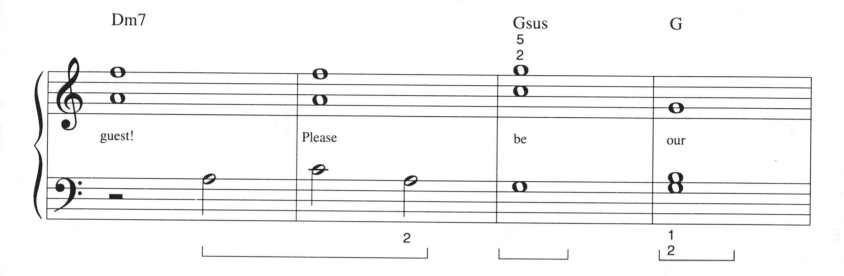

# SOMETHING THERE

Lyrics by HOWARD ASHMAN
Music by ALAN MENKEN

Moderately slow

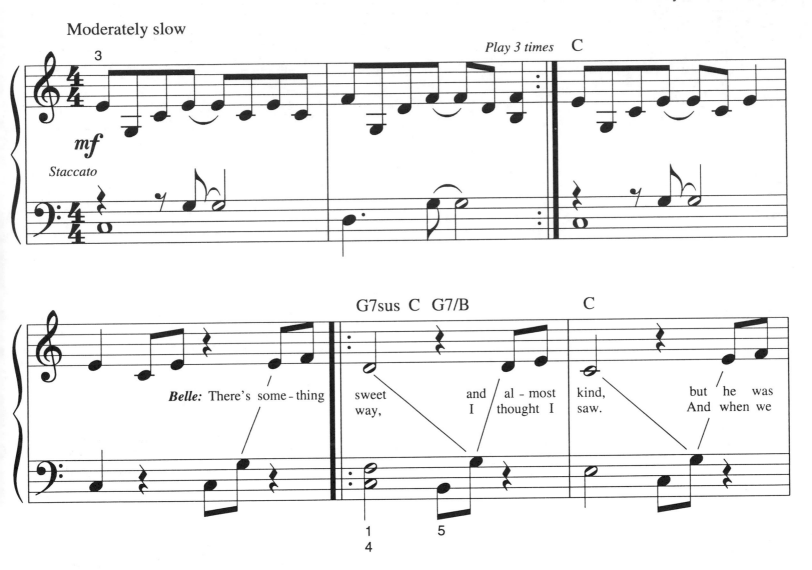

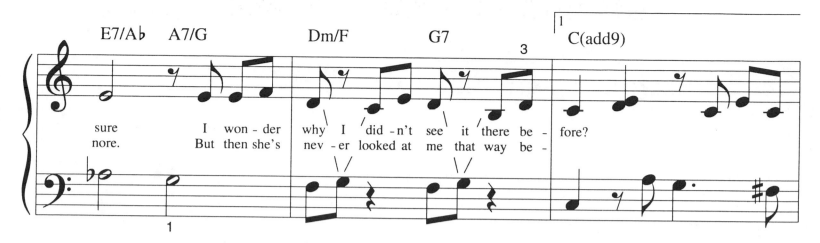

sure      I   won - der
nore.     But  then she's

why  I  did - n't  see  it  there be -
nev - er  looked at  me  that way be -

fore?

*Beast:* She glanced this

fore.

48

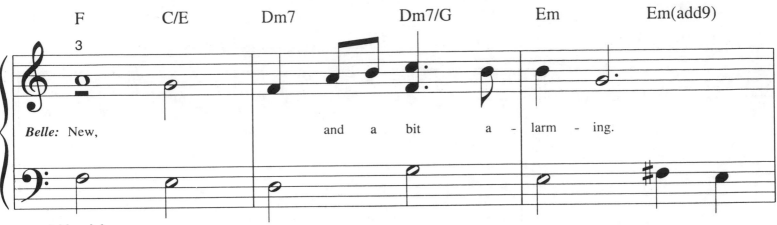

*Belle:* New,

and a bit a - larm - ing.

*Add pedal*

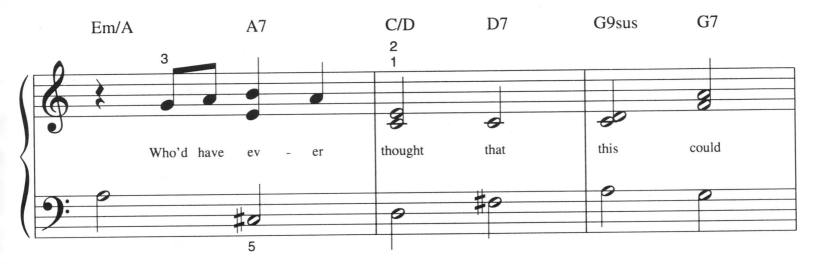

Who'd have ev - er thought that this could

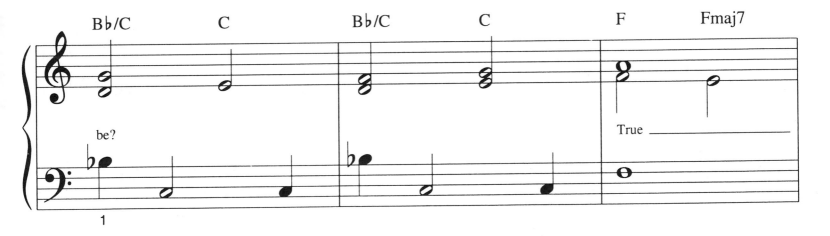

be?

True _____

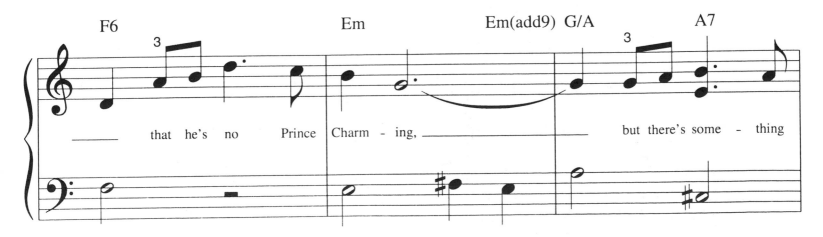

_____ that he's no Prince Charm - ing, _____ but there's some - thing

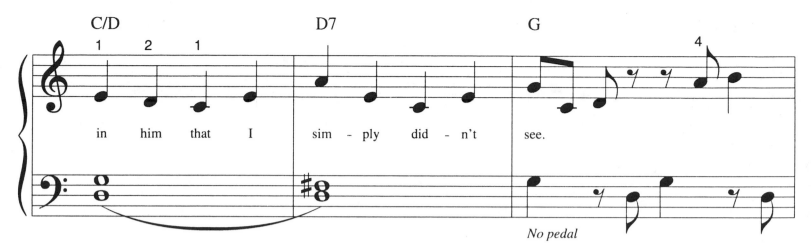

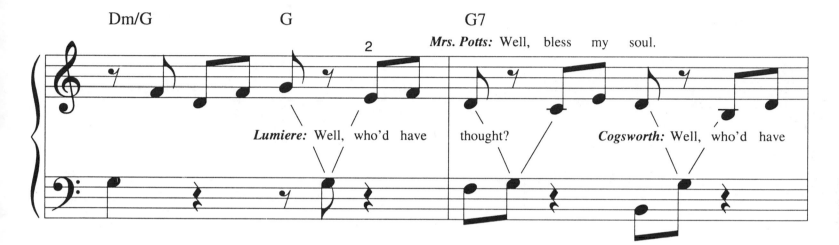

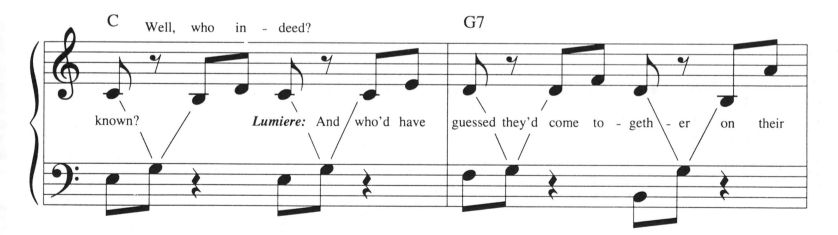

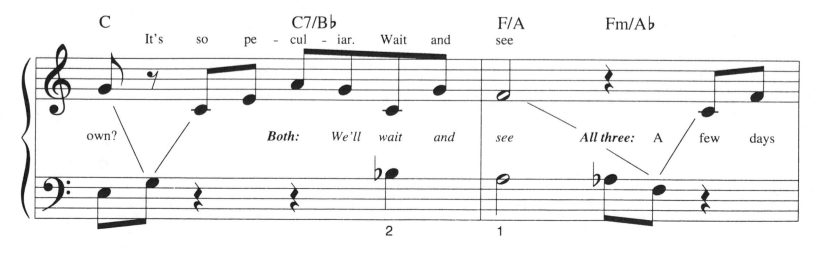

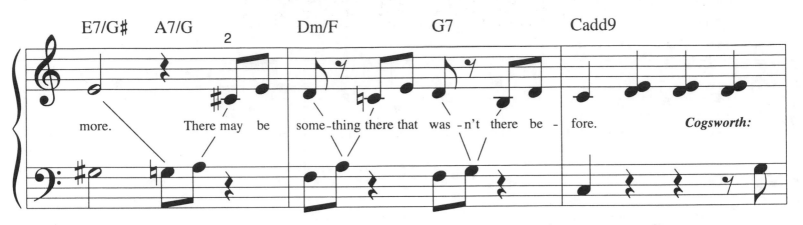

more. There may be some-thing there that was-n't there be - fore. *Cogsworth:*

*(You know, perhaps there's something there that)* was-n't there be - fore.

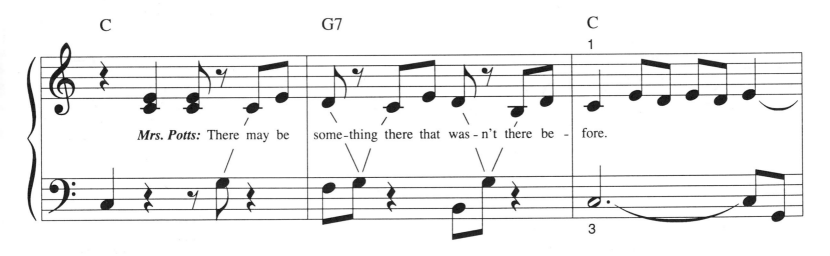

*Mrs. Potts:* There may be some-thing there that was-n't there be - fore.

*rit.*

# THE MOB SONG

Lyrics by HOWARD ASHMAN
Music by ALAN MENKEN

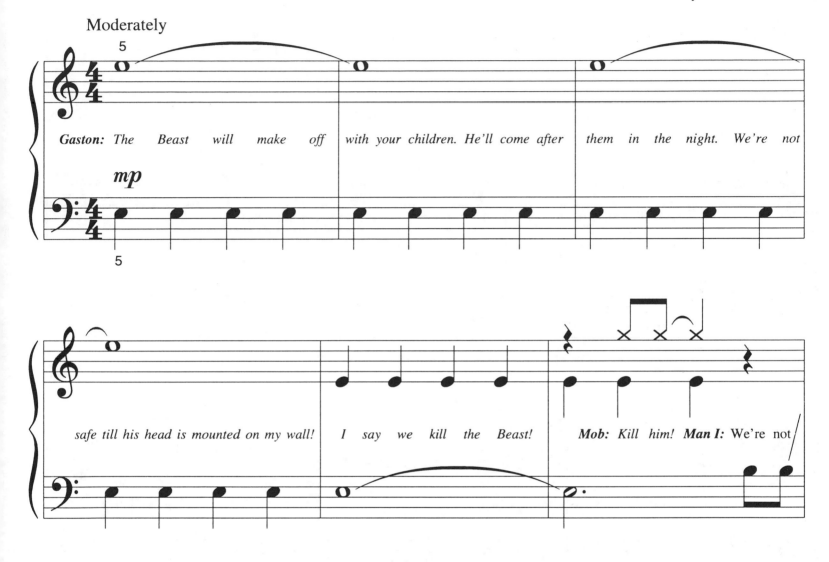

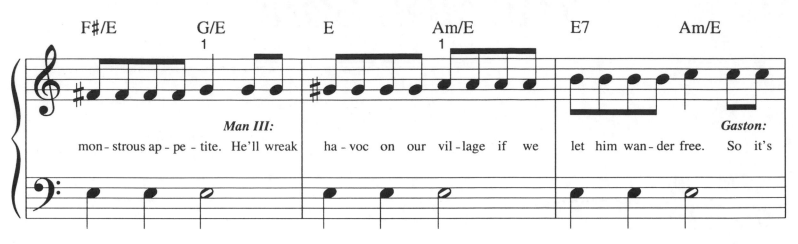

F#/E     G/E        E     Am/E       E7     Am/E

*Man III:*
mon-strous ap - pe - tite. He'll wreak ha - voc on our vil -lage if we let him wan - der free. So it's *Gaston:*

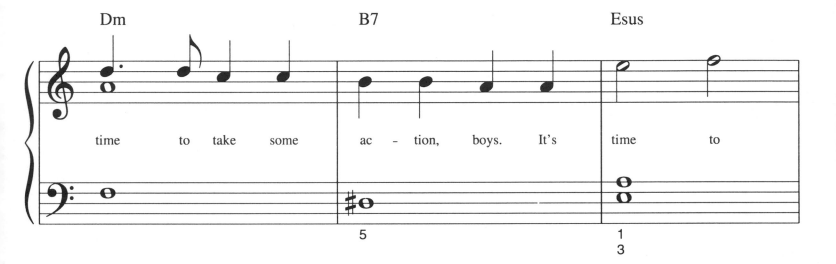

Dm              B7             Esus

time    to    take    some     ac - tion, boys. It's    time     to

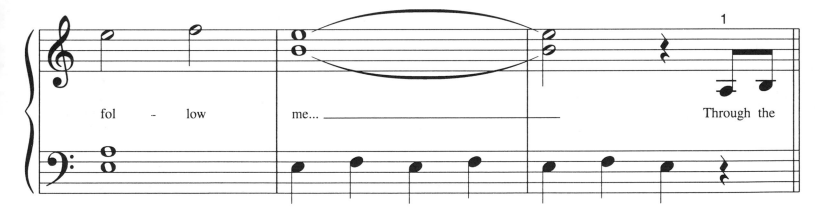

fol - low     me... _____       Through the

Am

mist, through the woods, through the dark-ness and the shad-ows. It's a night-mare but it's one ex-cit-ing
*Gaston:*                       *Mob:*
torch. Mount your horse. Screw your cour-age to the stick-ing place! We're count-ing on Gas-ton to lead the

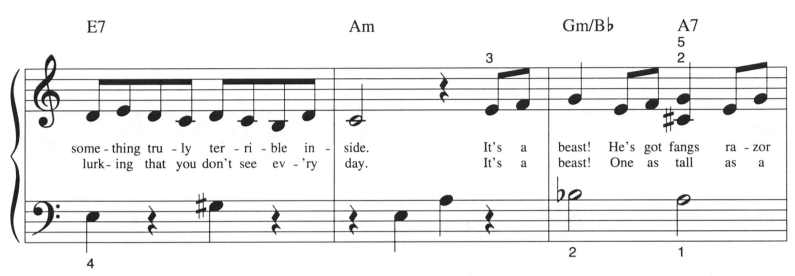

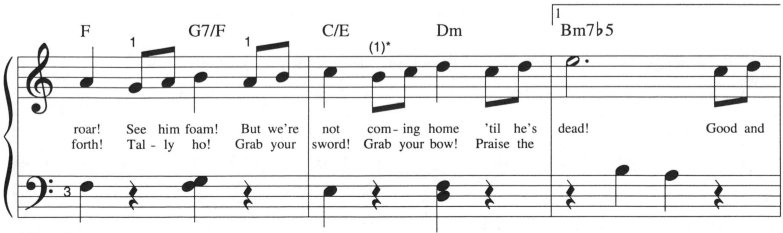

*Second time*

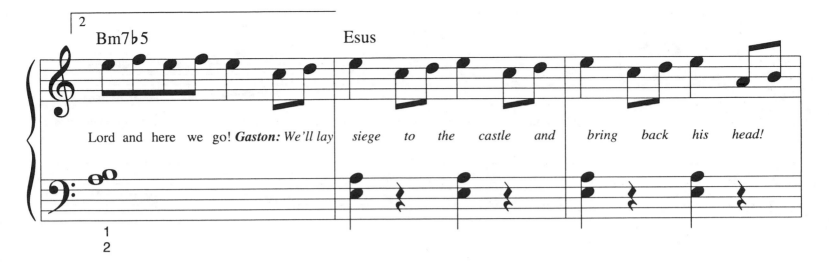

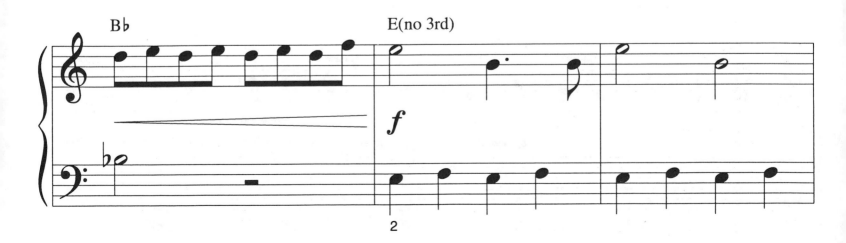

**Am**

We don't like what we don't un-der-stand in fact, it scares us and this

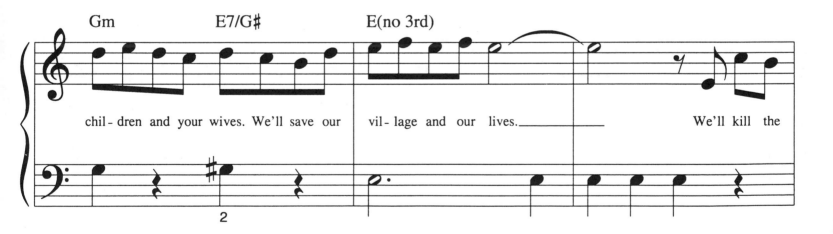

**Bb/A**     **E7**    **E7sus/F#**

mon-ster is mys-ter-i-ous at least. Bring your guns, bring your knives, save your

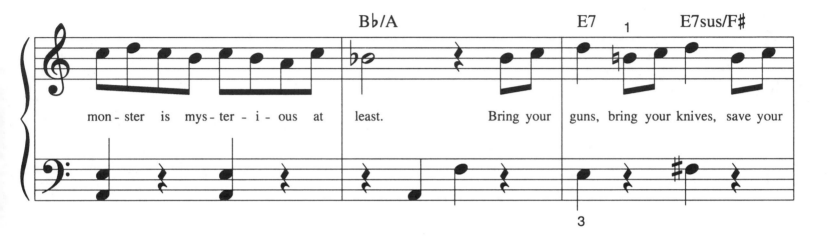

**Gm**     **E7/G#**     **E(no 3rd)**

chil-dren and your wives. We'll save our vil-lage and our lives._____ We'll kill the

**Am**

Beast! *Cogsworth: I knew it! I knew it was* *foolish to get our hopes up.* **Lumiere:**

Bb/A     E7     E7sus/F#

*Maybe it would have been better if she had never come at all. Could it be?* **Mrs. Potts:** *Is it she?*

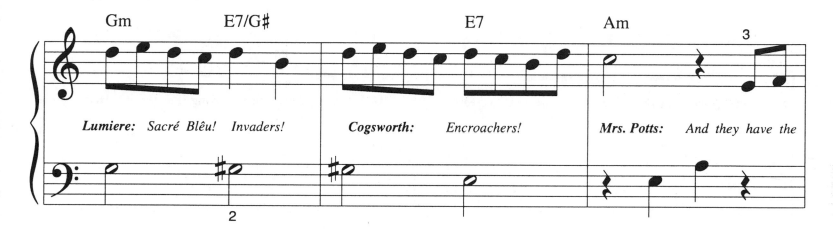

Gm     E7/G#     E7     Am

**Lumiere:** *Sacré Blêu! Invaders!* **Cogsworth:** *Encroachers!* **Mrs. Potts:** *And they have the*

Em7b5     A7     Dm     Em7b5     A7

*mirror!* **Cogsworth:** *Warn the Master! If it's a fight they want, we'll be ready for them!*

Dm     Bm7b5     E7     E(no 3rd)

*Who's with me?* **Gaston:** *Take whatever booty you can find. But remember,*

*the Beast is mine!* **Objects:** Hearts a - blaze, ban-ners high, we go march-ing in-to bat-tle un-a-

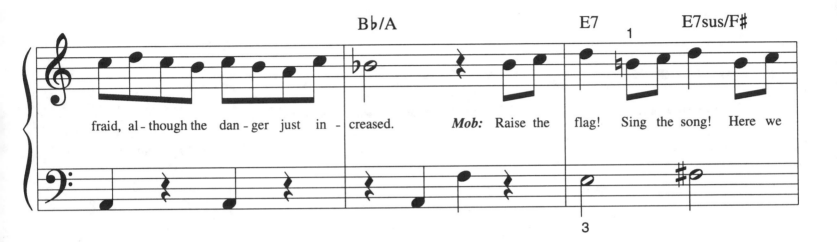

fraid, al-though the dan-ger just in-creased. **Mob:** Raise the flag! Sing the song! Here we

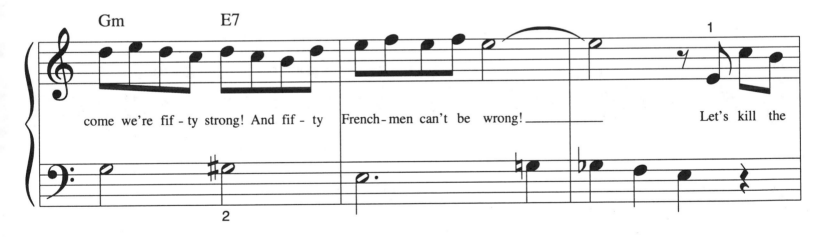

come we're fif-ty strong! And fif-ty French-men can't be wrong!_____ Let's kill the

Beast!

*mp*

*Add pedal*

**Mrs. Potts:** *Pardon me, Master.* **Beast:** *Leave me in peace.* **Mrs. Potts:** *But sir, the castle*

# BEAUTY AND THE BEAST

Lyrics by HOWARD ASHMAN
Music by ALAN MENKEN

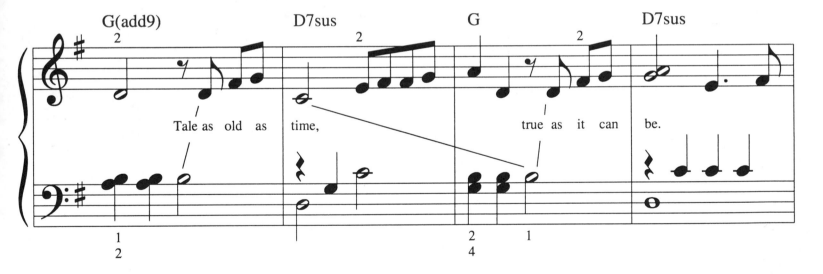

Tale as old as time, true as it can be.

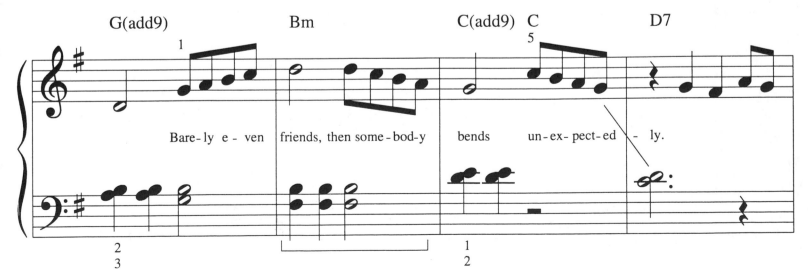

Bare-ly e-ven friends, then some-bod-y bends un-ex-pect-ed - ly.

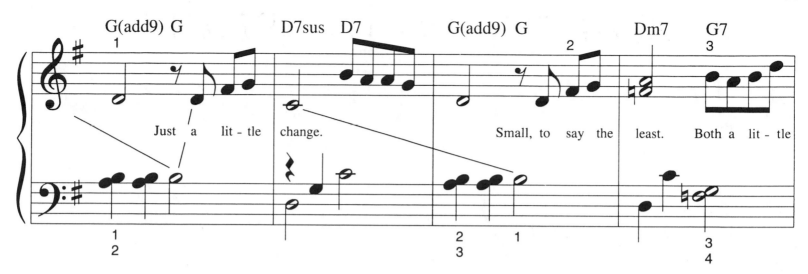

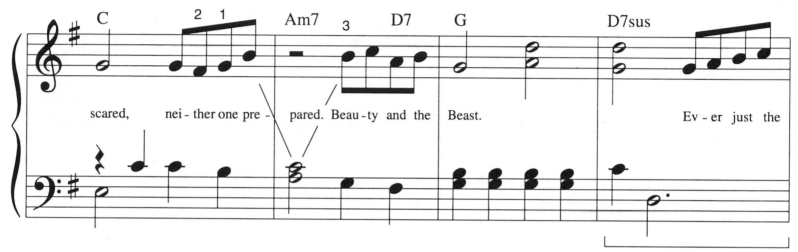

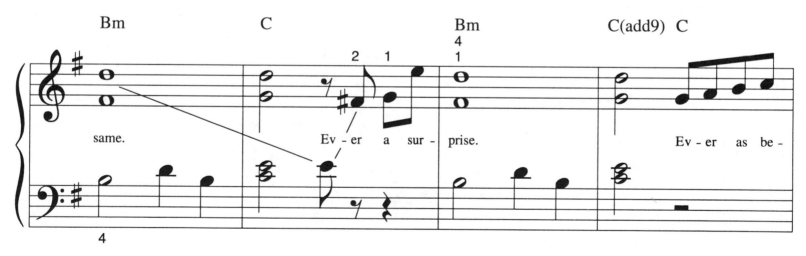

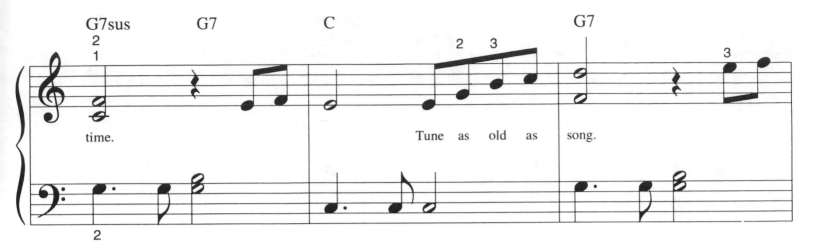

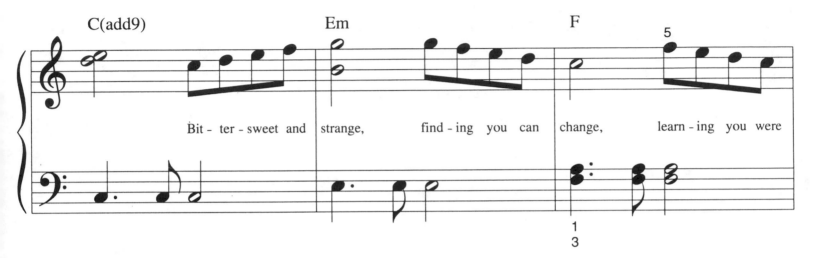

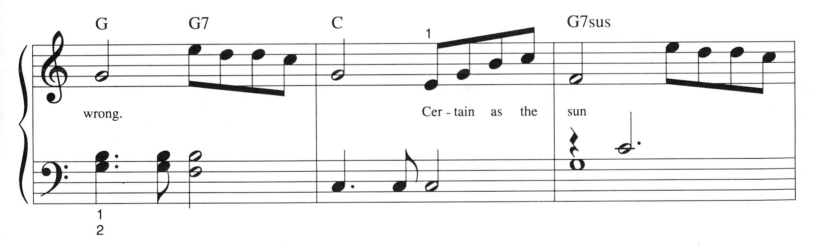

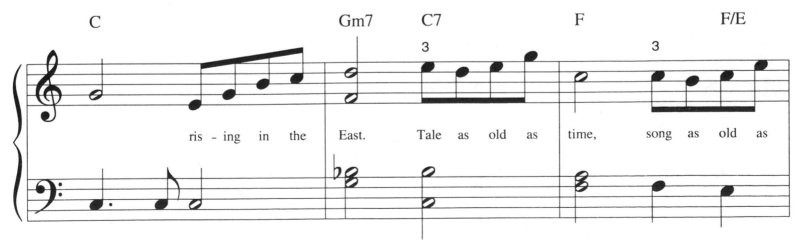

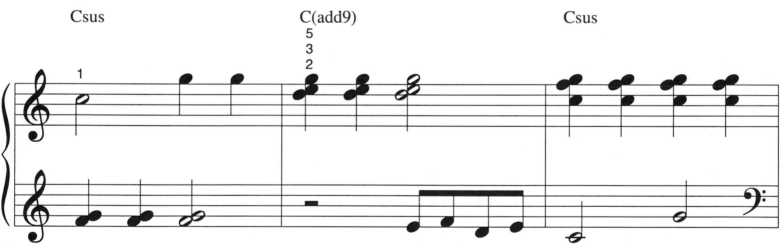

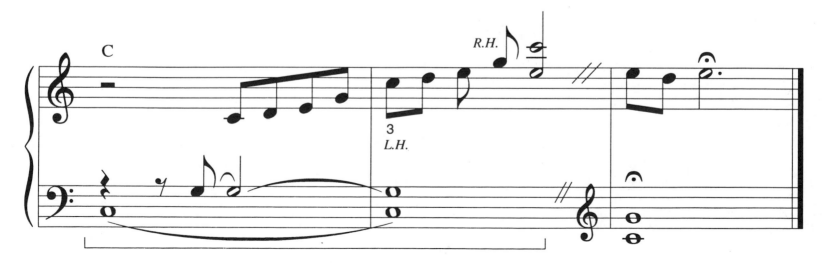